USING THIS BOOK

*One of the best ways of helping children to learn to read is by reading stories to them and with them. This way they learn what **reading** is, and they will gradually come to recognise many words, and begin to read for themselves.*

First, grown-ups read the story on the left-hand pages aloud to the child.

You can reread the story as often as the child enjoys hearing it. Talk about the pictures as you go.

Later the child is encouraged to read the words under the pictures on the right-hand page.

The pages at the back of the book will give you some ideas for helping your child to read.

British Library Cataloguing in Publication Data

McCullagh, Sheila K.
  Jeremy Mouse and Mr. Puffle. — (Puddle Lane.
  Stage 1; v.14)
  I. Title   II. Morris, Tony   III. Series
  823'.914[J]   PZ7
  ISBN 0-7214-0921-0

First edition

Published by Ladybird Books Ltd Loughborough Leicestershire UK
Ladybird Books Inc Lewiston Maine 04240 USA

Jeremy Mouse and Mr Puffle

written by SHEILA McCULLAGH
illustrated by TONY MORRIS

This book belongs to:

Ladybird Books

If you have not read **The Wideawake Mice**,
read this page first.

The Wideawake Mice were toy mice,
in Mr Wideawake's toy shop.
One evening, a magician came into
the shop.
He didn't see the Wideawake Mice,
but he spilt some magic dust
all over them.
That night, when the moon shone down,
the Wideawake Mice came alive.
They escaped from the shop
through a hole under the door, and
ran across the square to the market.
They climbed up a post and found
a safe place to live on a shelf
under the roof.

This story tells you about
what happened to Jeremy Mouse,
when he met Mr Puffle.

the Wideawake Mice

Jeremy Mouse woke up.
It was still dark in the shadows
under the roof,
but the sun was shining down on
the square outside the market building.

Jeremy Mouse
woke up.

Jeremy went to the edge of the shelf,
and looked down into the market below.
There were people in the market.
They had set up tables all around
the wall, and piled the tables
with good things to eat.

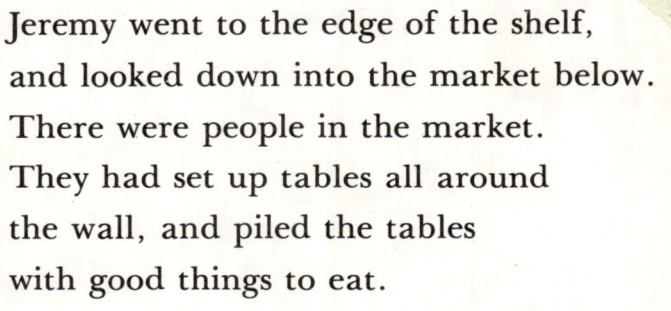

Jeremy Mouse
looked down.

Jeremy felt very hungry.
He was just going to climb down a post,
when someone behind him said,
"Who are you? And whatever
are you doing in those clothes?"

Jeremy looked up. He saw a mouse
looking out of a hole over his head.
"I'm Jeremy," he said.
"I always wear clothes.
I'm a Wideawake Mouse,
from Mr Wideawake's toy shop."

Jeremy looked up.
He saw a mouse.

The little mouse climbed down
on to the shelf beside Jeremy.
"You won't be wide awake very long,
if you wear things like that," he said.
"You'll never be able to run fast enough,
if Tom Cat sees you."

Jeremy looked down at his clothes.
"Do you think I should take them off?"
he said.

"I should," said the little mouse.
"Tom Cat could catch hold of them.
And then where would you be?"

"I don't know," said Jeremy.
"Where would I be?"

Jeremy and the
little mouse

"I'll tell you," said the mouse.
"You'd be inside Tom Cat,
before you could squeak twice.
I'm Chestnut Mouse, and I know."

Jeremy pulled off his clothes.
"It **does** feel better without them,"
he said.
"It's much safer," said Chestnut.

Jeremy pulled off
his clothes.

"Do you live here?" asked Jeremy.
"No," said Chestnut.
"I live in the Magician's garden,
at the end of Puddle Lane.
But I always come here on Fridays.
They have cheese and nuts
in the market on Fridays.
Come and see."

Jeremy looked down.
He looked at one of the tables.
There was a big cheese
at one end of the table,
and a basket of nuts
at the other end.

Jeremy looked down.

Jeremy felt very hungry,
and he could smell lovely smells
coming up from the market below.
Chestnut ran down a post,
and Jeremy followed him.

Chestnut and Jeremy
ran down a post.

"Keep close to me," whispered Chestnut.
"It can be dangerous down here."
He led the way along by the wall,
and under the table.
Jeremy saw two big feet
standing not far away.
Jeremy didn't know it, but
the two big feet belonged to Mr Puffle.
(Mr Puffle lived in Puddle Lane.)

Jeremy saw
two big feet.

Mr Puffle was buying some cheese.
The man at the table cut off
a big slice of cheese for Mr Puffle.
A crumb of cheese broke off.
It rolled off the table, and
fell on Mr Puffle's foot.

The cheese fell
on Mr Puffle's foot.

Mr Puffle's foot was close to Jeremy's nose.
Jeremy smelt the cheese.
He ran up on to Mr Puffle's foot,
and began to eat it.

Jeremy ran up
on to Mr Puffle's foot.

Mr Puffle looked down, and saw
Jeremy Mouse on his shoe.
Mr Puffle gave a great shout.
Jeremy was very frightened.
He hid under Mr Puffle's trouser leg.

Mr Puffle looked down,
and saw Jeremy Mouse.
Jeremy hid.

Mr Puffle gave another shout.
"There's a mouse on my foot!
There's a mouse on my foot!"
he cried.
"He's hiding under my trousers!"
Mr Puffle hopped about on one foot,
waving his other foot in the air.

Mr Puffle hopped
on one foot.

Jeremy was very frightened.
He saw Mr Puffle's leg.
He thought Mr Puffle's leg
looked just like a post,
so he ran up the leg
to Mr Puffle's knee.

Jeremy ran
up Mr Puffle's leg.

Mr Puffle gave another great shout.
"It's run up my leg!" he cried.
"It's run up my leg!"

"Shake your leg!"
cried the man with the cheese.
"Shake your leg hard!"

Mr Puffle hopped about on one foot,
shaking his other leg.

Mr Puffle hopped
on one foot.

Mr Puffle shook so hard,
that Jeremy had to let go.
He fell down Mr Puffle's leg,
and landed on his shoe.

Jeremy fell
down Mr Puffle's leg.

Mr Puffle saw Jeremy Mouse
on his shoe.
He gave a great kick.
Jeremy flew.
He flew through the air,
and landed on top of the low wall
around the market.

Jeremy flew.

As quick as a flash,
Jeremy ran up the post.
He hid in the dark on the shelf.

Jeremy ran up the post,
and hid.

"What **are** you doing, Jeremy?"
said a voice behind him.
Jeremy looked around.

It was Grandmother Mouse.
"I was hungry," said Jeremy.
"I went down to get something to eat.
It was very exciting."

"I expect it was,"
said Grandmother Mouse.
"A bit **too** exciting.
We'll go down tonight,
when the people have gone.
That's the best time
for a mouse to be in the market."

Jeremy and
Grandmother Mouse

Look at the pictures.
What is Chestnut doing?

Chestnut Mouse

Notes for the parent/teacher

Turn back to the beginning, and print the child's name in the space on the title page, using ordinary, not capital letters.

Now go through the book again. Look at each picture and talk about it. Point to the caption below, and read it aloud yourself.

Run your finger along under the words as you read, so that the child learns that reading goes from left to right.

Encourage the child to read the words under the illustrations. Don't rush in with the word before he/she has had time to think, but don't leave him/her struggling.

Read this story as often as the child likes hearing it. The more opportunities he/she has of looking at the illustrations and **reading** the captions with you, the more he/she will come to recognise the words.

If you have several books, let the child choose which story he/she would like.

Mrs Pitter-... dropped the tail with a ... She made such a noise, that she woke Mr Gotobed, who was fast asleep in bed in the house at the end of the lane.

Mr Gotobed woke up.